Little and Big

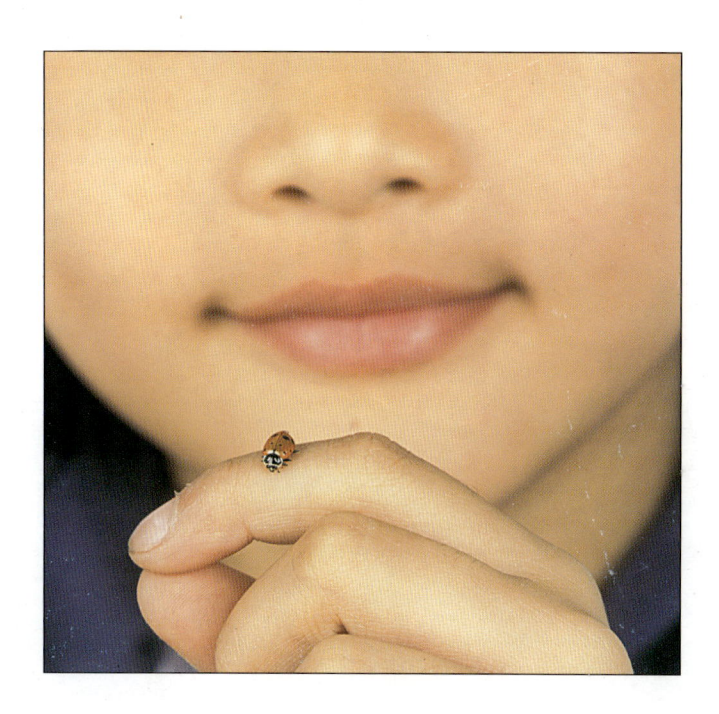

Christine Finochio • Jennette MacKenzie

This is a little tooth.

This is a big tooth.

This is a little foot.

This is a big foot.

This is a little eye.

This is a big eye.

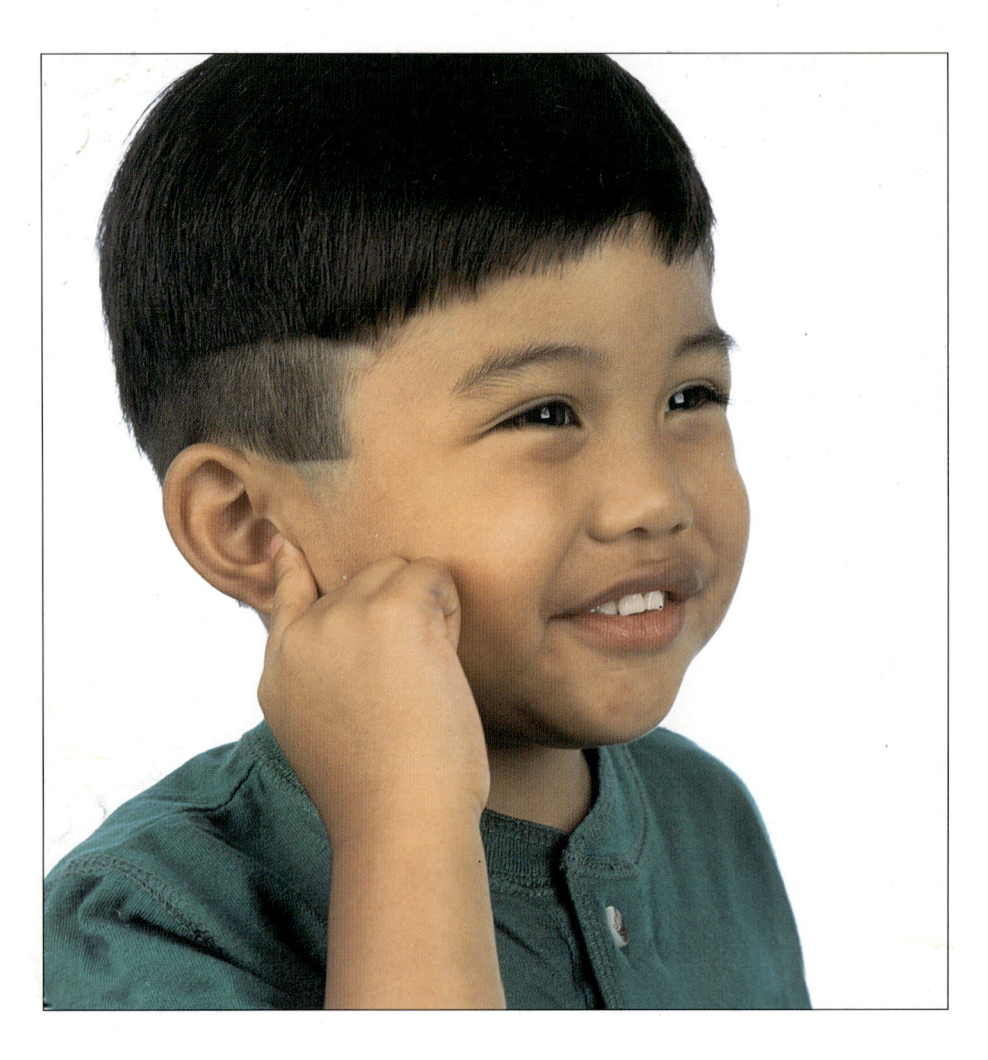

This is a little ear.

This is a big ear.

This is a little nose.

This is a big nose.

This is a little hand.

This is a big hand.

This is a little leg.

This is a big leg.

I am big.

This bug is little.